KU-594-349

Contents

For Shirley

A Guide to the

Photography of Church Furnishings

by
Richard S. Brun

CHURCH HOUSE
PUBLISHING

The Council for the Care of Churches acknowledges
with grateful thanks sponsorship of this book by
the Ecclesiastical Insurance Group.

ECCLESIASTICAL
INSURANCE GROUP
INSURANCE YOU CAN BELIEVE IN

Church House Publishing
Church House
Great Smith Street
London SW1P 3NZ

ISBN 0 7151 7577 7

Published 1999 by Church House Publishing

Printed in England by the University Printing House, Cambridge

List of illustrations

Preface

The author of this guide has been described as a 'photographic fanatic'. While still at school he ran a developing and printing service for his fellow pupils, and later worked as a darkroom assistant in a press agency. During regular service in the army, he acted as photographer to the 2nd Infantry Division until his demobilisation. He then served as a police officer, spending over ten years in his force's photographic unit; during this time he photographed 167 murder investigations. Before his unit was civilianised, he was responsible for all the negatives used in the invention of the now famous 'Photo-Fit' facial identification system. After leaving the photographic unit, he continued to specialise in observational and recording photography within the police service until his retirement, due to ill-health, in 1984. During his working life he also acted as an adviser on photography to a number of museums, businesses and other institutions, and also formed a collection of photographica that is now housed in a purpose-built gallery in a provincial museum. He lives with his wife in an isolated rural hamlet in Kent and, although confined to a wheelchair, still writes on both photographic topics and railway modelling. He is currently engaged on producing a photographic record of rural railway stations in the South-east of England.

Introduction

As outlined in my earlier booklet *Church Security: A Simple Guide* (published by the Council for the Care of Churches, 1989), there are a number of good reasons why church furnishings should be photographically recorded. If the recorded items should be stolen, the police will find a good photograph of the greatest help in tracing the whereabouts of the missing object. Many magazines and papers are happy to publish clear photographs of stolen items without charge, and at least one publication has a section exclusively devoted to the production of such photographs. Again, when a valuable item has been taken, the insurance loss adjuster often relies on photographs to assist him in accurately assessing the item's value in order to recommend a realistic settlement under the terms of an insurance policy. Lastly, good and clear photographs can more than help when an item has to be repaired or restored after some accidental damage, or a complete and identical replacement has to be sought after a loss due to damage or theft.

Most of these reasons for having photographs of church furnishings are well known and appreciated, but unfortunately many attempts to photograph various items end in failure, or the final results are later found to be virtually worthless as an accurate record of an item's individual characteristics. All too often, smaller items are photographed in groups: if only one or two from that group are later stolen, trying to make enlargements of those items from a small negative area of a sufficient quality to enable satisfactory reproduction can be a difficult and time-consuming business, and may indeed be impossible. It is an exercise that all too often an investigating police service has neither the time, the staff nor the finance to undertake. It is imperative that each item is photographed individually, and in the clearest and most detailed manner possible.

Of course, this type of photography is rather different from the usual family snapshots and holiday souvenirs that the majority of amateur photographers are used to undertaking. Even with the most modern of self-loading, self-focusing, automatic cameras now available to the more enthusiastic amateur photographers, most of their users have neither the knowledge nor the experience to be able to undertake accurately and easily this branch of photography. This guide is therefore designed to assist in the easy application of some professional methods by the average amateur photographer who wishes to use his equipment within the church recording context.

1

Equipment

■ Camera

The most important piece of equipment is, naturally, the camera. For this type of work, a 35mm single lens reflex (SLR) is ideal, for when framing the shot and focusing, the user is looking directly through the camera lens at the subject; with other camera types the operator has to use a separate viewfinder, which immediately causes problems of parallax and precise focusing, because it uses a slightly different viewpoint than that seen by the camera's taking lens. Even the close-focusing facility of the modern and popular compact camera is not close or accurate enough to be used for this type of recording work. Most keen amateur photographers will already possess a 35mm single lens reflex camera; if not, it is advised that one be purchased especially for the task.

This purchase need not be expensive; as well as using my own advanced camera outfit for the photographs used for this guide, I also purchased two second-hand cameras and used them alongside my usual camera. The first was a Russian-made Zenith single lens reflex camera, with a simple but effective built-in light meter, which at the time of writing (January 1996) cost £22 for a near mint example (see Fig.1). The second was a Pentax model K1000, which has a more advanced 'through the lens' light meter – that is, it measures only the light for the exposure after it has travelled through the taking lens. A mint condition example cost £115. Both cameras were fitted with a standard 50mm lens with a maximum aperture in each case of f.2. I have not indicated in the guide which camera was used in taking which illustration, it thus being apparent that all the

FIG. 1 A Zenith 11 camera purchased for £22, shown mounted with the battery powered video lamp. This lamp cost, in January 1996, £39.50.

cameras used are capable of producing work of a sufficiently high standard for magazine, book or other reproduction. Many other camera makes and models are available second-hand, and with care in their selection, all are suitable for the types of photographic tasks described in the guide. My own camera is an automatically focusing state-of-the-art body designed for hard and daily use, and for this guide was used only with a 50mm f1.4 lens.

When buying a second-hand camera, it is advisable to use an established dealer who will usually give a short guarantee with such items. Choose a camera that is clean inside and out, and which has no signs of damage or heavy wear; make sure that the battery compartment has no sign of any corrosion – if it has, reject it immediately. Over 75 per cent of camera breakdowns are caused by stale batteries that have been left in the camera and then leak. It should be noted that 'leak proof' batteries will leak if left overlong in a camera when they are exhausted! If the camera is clean inside and out, then make sure that the shutter release is smooth and quiet at a variety of speeds, and that the focusing movement on the lens is smooth and not tight and without any areas of harshness. Remember that a recent survey by a major film manufacturer showed that the average amateur photographer uses less than three films annually; so the chances are that even a ten-year-old camera will have taken fewer than one thousand exposures. The design life of most manually-operated cameras is 100,000 exposures before breakdown, so second-hand purchases of popular cameras should prove advantageous. The current modern designs of fully automatic motorised reflex cameras are proving equally hard-wearing but, if contemplating such a camera, try to select one that allows both manual focusing of a lens and some self-selection of the aperture and shutter speed.

■ Lens

The choice of lens is also quite important. Perhaps the best type is a 'macro' lens, specially made for use at close distances to a subject. These lenses are very much more expensive than standard types, and it is not usually realistic to purchase one unless one wishes permanently to specialise in this type of photography. Most lenses fitted to the older type of cameras are of the prime (fixed) focal length such as the f2 50mm already mentioned, and are usually, regardless of make, of a very high optical standard. Most modern contemporary cameras are now sold with a zoom lens, and while these can give excellent results, some distortions can be noticeable when there is a straight edge near a side of the shot; and they also let through less light than a prime or non-zoom lens. It is also advisable to avoid using a very wide angle lens, as these are very much more difficult to use than a more standard focal length, and may give rise to some very odd results when used close to an object. All in all, the best results can most easily be obtained in this context with the standard 50mm lens fitted to a 35mm camera, which also has the advantage of being very much cheaper than other types and focal lengths of lenses! The most important thing to remember, when using any lens, is always to use a lens hood. This will not only protect the vulnerable front of the lens from knocks and marking, but by preventing extraneous light from reaching the lens, will do more to improve picture quality than any other lens attachment or camera accessory. It was not for nothing, and was perfectly true, when I was instructed over forty years ago that the use of a lens hood doubles the value of a lens!

■ Film

It now remains to consider the type (not make) of film that is suitable for this type of work. Films are manufactured in two main types: positive is used to produce slides, and negative is used to produce prints. The Council for the Care of Churches recommends that the latter is used, so that it is possible to look at an item in the *Church Property Register* (formerly known as the *Terrier*) and see what it looks like without recourse to a slide projector. Moreover, it is easier to store and protect a negative and prints than a single transparency. Films are sold with differing amounts of sensitivity to light, which is normally

Warranty details inside
Détails de garantie à l'intérieur

Recycled cardboard
Carton recyclé

ISO 100/21°
PROCESS AP 70/C 41

27 Exp. **DX** Agfa-Gevaert AG
24 x 36 mm   D-51301 Leverkusen · Postfach 10 01 60
Made in Germany

Process before
Zu entwickeln bis
A développer avant
Revelar antes de   4363 30 01/98

FIG. 2 Film box showing the ISO rating, the number of exposures that may be made on the film, the type of development process to be used by the processing laboratory, and the 'process before' date. The last is an advisory date of the expiry of the film's uniform standard of quality.

indicated by an ISO number that is printed on the box in which the film cassette is sold. The higher the number, the more sensitive to light the film is, and therefore the less exposure it will require for an accurate exposure at a given light level. This increased sensitivity is gained at the loss of some quality in the finished print, and very sensitive (or 'fast') films give a noticeable grain effect to the picture. We therefore have to balance a choice in sensitivity with the result we desire, and I would recommend that a film of a medium sensitivity be used; all the illustrations in this guide were taken using my 'standard' film choice, an Agfa film with an ISO rating of 200. A similarly rated film from any of the major manufacturers would give a similar result. A correctly exposed film will yield prints that also correctly depict the relationship of one colour with another; while we all see colours slightly differently from each other, most of us when looking at a colour photograph accept that the result is quite realistic. A further advantage in using colour negative material is that the film is easily obtained, and its processing is comparatively inexpensive and generally available. The final negative can also be used to produce a black-and-white print if required. Even the initial colour prints received from the processor can be reproduced satisfactorily in monochrome; as a practical demonstration of this, all the illustrations in the guide were reproduced direct from colour prints, and all the original film processing and printing was done in local high street stores. In other words, the author has used only the films and processing available to any member of the public, instead of the now all too commonplace practice in many guides of advising an amateur process, and then using specialized professional equipment and processing to provide the illustrations!

■ Camera support

In any serious photography, after the camera and lens, and the choice of film, the third most important part of the equipment is some means of holding the camera steady. Do not be tempted to think that your hands are so steady that you can dispense with a tripod or other means of support. Some years ago whilst lecturing to a course of trainee forensic photographers, I stated that no one can hand hold a camera steady enough for critical use, regardless of the shutter speed being used. A keen amateur photographer of many years' standing challenged me in this, and an experiment was set up. While my challenger took a hand-held exposure at 1/60th second, I took a second exposure with the same camera at the same exposure, using a tripod. The subsequent twenty diameter enlargements from the two negatives needed no guidance as to which was the hand-held exposure!

The simplest and cheapest form of camera support is a bean bag – a small version, in fact, of the popular chair cushion. The camera type can be purchased for a few pounds from virtually any camera store, but it is a simple task to run one up from any scrap material and fill it either with the expanded plastic 'beans' sold as a stuffing material, or to use dried peas or haricot beans. When used, the bag is placed on to a firm table or bench, and the camera is pressed into position in the centre of the bag; after framing and focusing, the camera shut-ter is released via a cable release, an electronic switch if the camera is a modern one, or by means of the camera's own delayed action release. For much simple work, this type of support is both cheap and efficient.

A proper tripod is, however, much to be preferred, and here it is essential that care is taken in the choice of purchase. There are many lightweight tripods available, some of them for less than £25, and while suitable for occasional holiday use, they are not really ideal for serious use of a camera for recording work. A tripod should above all be stable under all conditions, and it is here that weight is important – the heavier the tripod is, the better and more vibration-free it is. A lighter type of tripod will vibrate at any puff of wind, or even a passing footfall. My tripod can rise to a height of two and a half metres, and support any camera (or projector) at that height, while still being able to hold a camera a few centimetres from the floor. Many of the professional types of tripod appear second-hand, and they are worth looking out for. Whether the tripod is fitted with a substantial ball-and-socket head or the more common pan-and-tilt head is a matter of personal choice, but do make sure that whatever type you select, it can be locked solidly in a chosen position. And remember, whenever you operate a camera on a tripod, do not spoil the support offered by the tripod and release the shutter by hand; always use a cable release, or the built-in delayed action device.

■ Numbering system

When several photographs are being taken within a church, a numbering system should be used for each exposure, ideally tied in with the order of the furnishings in the *Church Property Register*. Thus the photograph of an object would show the same number as the description of that object in the *Register*, keeping any likelihood of an error in an object's identification to a minimum. The number must be clearly visible on the finished print. A simple system could make use of moulded plastic numerals, as sold by most model shops, held on simple plastic rods; even cheaper are the rub-down printed numbers such as 'Letraset' or similar, placed on to folded white card. Now that many people have access to a personal computer or word processor, suitable numbers in some larger size could be printed off, then put on to small cards next to the object being photographed. Last, and easiest, is to use a large felt-tipped marker pen and write directly on to a card at the time the photograph is taken – as long as the writer can produce a neat and legible numeral, for it is no use 'spoiling the ship for a ha'p'orth of tar', and putting a hastily scrawled number into a perfectly exposed and composed photograph! It is not generally a good idea to include a ruler in the photograph to indicate the object's size, as it is difficult to find a rule or scale that is sufficiently legible to be easily read in the finished print. It also adds to the photographer's problems trying to make sure that the subject is correctly lit, the index number is in the shot and focused, and that the rule is vertical, visible and also focused. In any correctly-made inventory, the measurements of the article should be fully and accurately described, making a

Fɪɢ. 3 Numbers (from left to right) written on card, using moulded plastic numerals, and a number card printed on a computer system.

visual guide in the photograph superfluous. The only time that an indexing number need not be included in the photograph at the time of exposure is when the large size of an object itself makes that difficult; examples would include larger items of furniture or windows, where the card or number display is rendered too small to be seen in the camera viewfinder, or indeed, in the final print.

■ Finished print

Before moving on to consider the practical aspects of recording photography, there is one last detail to be considered – that of the finished print. When taking a film to be processed, tell the shopkeeper or dealer that you require the larger of whatever print sizes you are offered. Some processors offer a 'super' sized print at the same or slightly higher price as a standard sized print. Additionally, an increasing number of processors can also offer a print size of five inches by seven inches for only £1 or so extra. This is certainly a bargain, as almost the whole area of a 35mm negative is printed, and the finished print is appreciably larger than even a so-called 'super print' size. In fact, I always have films printed to a 5 by 7 format, and currently the extra cost is only 50p a film, and this from a mail order processor! However, what is of great importance is the type of print finish that is stipulated. It is essential that prints are finished as *glossy* prints, regardless of any personal preferences of the photographer or churchwarden. While many prefer a matt or silk finish to their prints, these finishes can seriously interfere with the reproduction process should the photograph need to be circulated in a newspaper or magazine. Examine a matt or especially a silk finished print through a magnifying glass, and you will see that the print surface has a fine texture embossed on to it; it is this texture that interferes with the block-making process, and it also spoils the clarity of information which can be obtained by an expert critically examining the image of the item in such a photograph.

To sum up, the main points regarding the selection of

equipment and ancillary items as mentioned so far in the text are:

- ❏ Select the correct type of camera for the task in hand, preferably a 35mm SLR.
- ❏ Try and use a standard 50mm lens fitted with a lens hood.
- ❏ Use a fresh medium speed negative type film.
- ❏ Ensure the camera is used only on a stable and firm support, such as a tripod.
- ❏ Make the exposure by using a cable release or a delayed action release.
- ❏ Ensure that a numbering system will be clearly visible in the finished print.
- ❏ Stipulate to the processor that gloss finished prints are required.

2

Techniques used in church recording photography

The principal technique that I have evolved when taking photographs within a building as part of a recording process is that of using, whenever possible, the available natural light as my sole or main illumination source. The use of simpler flash equipment in this context can give rise to more problems than it solves; certainly the use of a camera's own built-in flash unit is not recommended under any circumstances. Remember, we are not talking here about taking one or two carefully staged and lit studio pictures, but of taking perhaps dozens of shots in a single session, in a location that may not possess an electric power supply. I was once called upon to photograph the entire contents of two galleries in a specialised provincial museum, the photographs being required by an insurance company before they would provide renewal of the insurance policy. In only ten working days a total of 1688 items were individually photographed, and a 10 x 8 inch print produced from every negative; all the exposures were made using the available and existing light in the galleries, using various mirrors and cards as light reflectors.

Most buildings contain sufficient light during daylight hours for careful photography. Even in the darkest corner, only a little artificial light need be supplied, as long as it is evenly applied. Again, I have found that the light from an ordinary 'Anglepoise' type desk lamp with a blue so-called 'daylight' bulb is perfectly adequate, especially if the camera lens is fitted with a Wratten 85B type filter in order to correct the colour balance of the light. Incidentally, if photographing under fluorescent light, fit your camera lens with FL-D type correction filter to remove the excessive green cast this form of popular lighting causes. Both types of filter are readily available from local photographic dealers at a cost of only a few pounds, and are commonly in screw mounts to fit the standard lens sizes. A more recently available source of good quality lighting is the re-chargeable video lamp; these again are available as part of a video camera outfit, and can also be purchased as an accessory from local camera and video dealers at reasonable cost – at the time of writing, one unit costs only £32 complete. The main drawback is that there is only sufficient power in the battery for a few minutes' continuous use.

While I intimated that simple flash units and built-in flash units should not be used, there are units available that can be used safely and without undue concern as to the results. The trouble with the simple units is that the light they produce is too near the optical centre of the lens on the camera, and this causes hot-spots of light to appear on the objects being photographed. Remember that even a polished oak coffer acts as a very efficient light reflector! The use of such flash units when photographing polished metal, such as a silver chalice, gives rise to unrecognisable prints that appear to be of the sun. But if the photographer owns, and has experience with, an advanced modern computer-linked flash unit, it can with care be used satisfactorily. Such units usually have a high power, but the flash head can be tilted and angled, and are of such a size that the light source is some way above the lens itself. Such flash units are usually sold by the makers of the camera themselves, and are designed to be used on that maker's cameras only; they link electronically to the camera's own exposure calculator system, and the units thereby become extremely flexible and accurate in use. Needless to say, they are also very expensive, and generally cost more than most even keen amateur photographers are prepared to spend on a camera alone.

When photographing portable objects, it is best if a fixed station is set up so that the plane of focus and lighting remain almost constant from item to item. If this can be conveniently

FIG. 4 An example of flash burn-out, caused by using a simple flash gun mounted above the camera lens.

arranged outdoors, so much the better, but try to avoid direct sunlight in a cloudless sky – fewer exposure problems will occur on a cloudy bright day. If a small but firm table is used as the support for the items to be photographed, a smaller but higher support should be provided immediately to its rear; the support table should be at right angles to the main source of the light, whether this is natural daylight or an artificial source. The rear support need be nothing more than a chair that is placed on another table, or a projector screen or other portable screen erected close to the main table. From the top of the support at the rear, a large piece of a neutral coloured material should be draped so as to hang down behind the items to be recorded, and also across the surface of the table surface on which they will stand. The material used should be fairly lightweight so as to fall easily into folds, and also to spread over the surface of the table in such a way as to achieve a continuous curve from the top of the rearmost support to about the centre of the support table. The idea of this is three-fold: it isolates the item being recorded from what may otherwise be a distracting background; it provides a common link from one photograph to another; and it also helps to achieve a constant exposure from one item to the next. The colour of the material is of greater importance than its weave; on no account fall into the common error of believing that a black cloth will be best, for that will adversely affect the initial correct exposure, and also cause difficulties in any subsequent reproduction process that may be required. Of course, any material with a noticeable pattern or design should be rejected. Ideally, material of a pastel colour should be obtained; I use a selection of such materials, all bought as remnants from local shops, including curtaining materials in pale tints of browns, greys, blues, and also a fine velvet in a washed-out green hue. Any strong colours should be avoided because they may cause a colour cast to be reflected across the object being recorded.

When photographing portable objects fairly closely, it is essential that the camera lens is accurately focused. The depth of focus in such circumstances is very shallow, and even when a

FIG. 5 A simply assembled set station, using a small table, stool and chair, with a cloth draped over. This set-up, facing a window, was used for the majority of the illustrations in the guide.

small aperture is selected in order to increase this depth, the whole field of sharp and exact focus may still be only a matter of a few millimetres. It is advisable therefore, that if a modern automatically focusing type of camera is used, the lens or camera control (depending on the model) should be disconnected so that manual focusing is used. This is because the sensors in such cameras will select the nearest point of an object on which to focus, thus making any reasonable depth impossible. Do not forget the 'rule of three' – by focusing on a plane about one third of the total width or diameter of an object from its front and using a medium aperture, the whole of the object can often be rendered in sharp focus. It is usual to compose the shot in the camera viewfinder, and then to focus manually on a 'target' held in the correct plane next to the subject. This need only be a printed card, book cover, or similar target that is held vertically and squarely to the camera, then removed once the plane of focus selected has been achieved. In difficult situations, such as photographing a lectern or a chair in a darkened corner, use a tape measure to find the focusing distance, and then transfer this measurement to the focusing scale engraved on the lens mount.

Before moving on to consider the methods used in photographing various classes of objects, the principles that govern exposures should be mentioned. The film, as mentioned earlier, has a measurement of its sensitivity notated by an ISO number. The system is a simple arithmetical one, so that a film having an ISO rating of 200 is twice as sensitive to light as one rated at 100, and half as sensitive as one rated at 400. Exactly the same relationship exists between aperture numbers – a lens set to f5.6 transmits twice as much light as one set to f8, and half as much as a lens set at f4. This holds good regardless of the make or the focal length of the lens; a lens set to an aperture of f5.6 will always transmit the same amount of light as any other lens that is also set at f5.6. Similarly, shutter speeds are arranged to give the same halving or doubling between adjacent settings. Setting a shutter speed of 1/60th second will allow half as much light through to the film as a shutter set at

Fig. 6 A modern advanced 35mm automatically focusing camera, fitted with a f1.4 prime lens and lens hood. The camera has a number of exposure modes, but can be operated completely manually. It is shown fitted with an advanced flash gun that has a swivelling and tilting head; it also can have its light output varied manually. Being controlled by an on-board computer, and also linked electronically to the camera computer, the flash is very flexible in use, and almost guarantees a correct exposure under almost any conditions. The cost of the camera, lens and flash shown (in 1996) is over £1325.

1/30th second. This relationship has been explained at some length because it often happens that in a darkened area such as the interior of a church, it becomes difficult for the camera meter to determine accurately an exposure – the light is outside the range of the meter at that particular combination of shutter speed, lens aperture and film sensitivity rating that has been set. Opening the lens to its maximum and slowing the shutter speed to its longest setting will often enable a reading to be obtained. Then by doubling the time that the shutter is to be held open for each whole aperture the lens is stopped down, a correct combination will be reached that allows the whole object to be sharply focused and correctly exposed. Many modern cameras will indeed indicate an exposure in very dark conditions, but this may be at an indicated aperture that is not suitable for the subject and its focus. In that case, switch the exposure mode to a manual or aperture priority one, and set the aperture first, then, if needed, adjust the shutter speed.

3

Methods of photographing church furnishings

■ Silverware and other polished metal

The main difficulty in photographing silverware (or any other shaped polished metal) is controlling the reflections on the object, which may range from the reflection of the camera itself on the surface, to dazzling reflections 'burning out' the detail or hiding the shape or decoration of the object's surface. It is essential that no flash photography is attempted, as this will give rise to too many uncontrollable reflections. Again, it is often mistakenly believed that silverware should be photographed against a black background, but this is definitely not so. A far better result will be more easily obtained if a light coloured background is used, as long as it has a fine weave or texture. The background should, of course, be out of focus, or in a soft focus; the object recorded will then stand out sharply with an added three-dimensional appearance in the finished print. In order to achieve a sharpness of focus over the whole visible surface of a piece of hollow-ware, such as a flagon, the point that is selected for focusing on should be one-third of the distance from the front of the item to its maximum diameter. All too often it will be found that if one focuses on the very front of the object, the sides will be softly depicted.

For many years, professional advice advocated photographing silver and other polished metal objects inside a 'tent', with lights arranged to shine on the sides of the tent, with the camera at one open end. There is no doubt that if a very great number of items need to be recorded, this method still has its place today. The tent can be constructed of simple light wooden laths, and the framework covered with a thin muslin-type material, or greaseproof paper. The sketch below will make the method clearer.

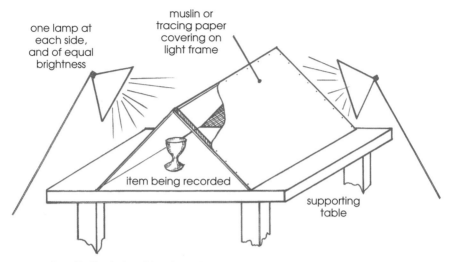

FIG. 7 Sketch of tent method of silverware photography

While the tent system does yield excellent results, it is a cumbersome and time-consuming method when only relatively few items – say, fewer than a couple of dozen – are to be recorded. For photographing items of silver individually, in the same way as other portable objects, a way of controlling individual reflections seen through the camera viewfinder must be used. One method, almost as old as photography itself, advocates spraying milk on to the object via a scent spray, but experience has shown this tends to be rather messy, haphazard in its results, and can also be rather smelly on hot days! It is possible now to purchase aerosols containing a special 'dulling' spray from specialist photographic dealers; when sprayed on to an item of polished metal, it makes the whole surface appear to have a matt finish. While it certainly controls all reflections, it can lead to the objects appearing rather flat in the finished print, and can also be very difficult to remove from intricate or detailed surfaces

A very simple and cheap method is to look through the focused camera's viewfinder at the object in the light that is used to make the exposure, and note where the points or areas of unwanted reflections are. Then, using a ball of soft 'Plasticine' or putty, dab the area in order to leave a small dulled area from the oil in the material. Areas causing the reflection can be treated so as to kill the offending glare or highlight effectively and safely and, after the item is photographed, the area can be gently repolished with a soft cloth without any undue effort.

Ideally, the exposure should be made using the available light at the time, even if this necessitates a time exposure. But this should not be all square to the object; as an aid in showing the shape of an item, one side should be slightly more brightly lit than the other. This is best and most easily achieved by using a plain white card as a reflector set up to one side, so as to reflect additional light on to the item. A very efficient and easily adjusted light reflector I have used for many years is a double-sided shaving mirror – try using both the plain and the concave sides in turn, for they give differing effects. Larger plain mirrors can also be used, although they invariably give difficulty in both supporting them and angling them in the correct position.

Objects that are visibly damaged, repaired or restored should ideally have the relevant area recorded in close-up. Such photographs are a very positive means of an object's identification, and can be of inestimable use in proving ownership, should that be contested after a recovery from a theft. Similarly, engraved wordings, armorials and hallmarks should also be recorded in close-up. In order to do so, the lens will need to have a supplementary lens screwed into its front mount, in the same way as a filter, in order to enable the lens to focus at a distance very much closer than normal. These lenses can be purchased very cheaply, either singly, or more commonly, in sets of three. They are in standard strengths, which are normally expressed in 'dioptres' – the higher the dioptre power, the closer the lens will enable the camera to be used to an object. In a set of three lenses, the powers are usually 1, 2 and 4 dioptres, so that combinations of lenses can

Fig. 8 Silver chalice, taken in available light, using a plain white
card as a reflector.

be used to increase the usefulness both of the lenses and of your camera. If a single lens is purchased, it is suggested that this be of two dioptres; this is sometimes marked as being 'No.2', rather than the dioptre power being engraved on the mount. While the lenses can be stacked to produce a very high power and therefore enable the camera to be used very close up indeed, resulting in quite a large image on the negative, this is not encouraged. It only requires a minute vibration in the camera to produce a blurred and useless image; also some distortion will be apparent in such examples in the corners of

Fɪɢ. 9 Close-up of a hallmark on a piece of silver, taken with a 35mm camera and a standard 50mm lens fitted with stacked supplementary lenses to a total power of six dioptres. The exposure was made in available light, aided by a concave shaving mirror to reflect light on to the immediate area being recorded.

the negative area. The use of supplementary lenses up to a total of about six dioptres is worthwhile, but larger amounts should be avoided, and are really unnecessary in recording silverware objects. Supplementary lenses are by far the cheapest and simplest method of enabling a camera to be used in a very close manner, especially as they are unique in that they do not require any exposure compensation to be applied. They can be used on any focal length of lens, and if used on a longer type of lens such as a 100 or 135 mm, quite large ratio enlargements can more easily be obtained than by other methods. But it is absolutely essential that the camera be used on a very firm support, and any possible vibration to affect either the camera or the subject is eliminated before the exposure is made.

The main points therefore to bear in mind when recording silver or other metal objects are:

❑ Use a light coloured background, definitely not black.
❑ Subdue the unwanted reflections with 'Plasticine' or similar material.
❑ Use available light aided by a reflector. Do not use any type of flash unit.
❑ Record in close-up any area of damage, or engraving and hallmarks, as additional photographs.

■ Glassware

When photographing glass furnishings such as water ewers, wine cruets, altar trays and candlesticks, reflections when controlled are important in showing both the shape and the decoration of an article. Again, the use of flash tends to create problems, not solving the exposure criteria. Photographing glassware is one of the very rare occasions when a black background can be used to advantage. However, a black cloth rarely achieves the correct appearance in the finished print; what should be used is a shadow box. This piece of apparatus has many uses in professional studios, where there is often a variety of shadow boxes of differing sizes ready for use, mainly of a wood construction, lined with velvet. For occasional use as envisaged here, a suitably prepared cardboard box is perfectly adequate. Preferably its depth should be greater than its width, but as long as the box has an opening large enough to contain comfortably the largest piece of glassware that you wish to record, all well and good.

Before use, the box will need to be prepared and converted from being a common container to being a piece of photographic equipment. The mouth of the box should be cleaned up, and any flaps carefully removed. Then, using a matt black car spray aerosol available at car assessory shops, coat the complete interior surface of the box; several coats may be needed before a uniform matt black finish is produced – it is important that *no* apparent sheen is visible on the painted surfaces. The box should be supported securely and level on a convenient table or stand, at a suitable height to enable work to be done without unduly bending one's back; remember, the photographer may have to spend quite a considerable time arranging and angling the items correctly in order to achieve the best results. The object to be photographed should then be placed just inside the box opening, and the lighting arranged to fall upon it from one side, at quite an oblique angle. If lighting is used from both sides equally, the object will appear in a flat and uninteresting manner. It is crucially important that no light is used from a source at the front of the box, for then the interior of the box will be lit, and will record as a shade of grey instead of a true dead black. This is true even if a velvet lined box is used; the blackness of the box's interior is the background to the item being recorded. The item should be rotated carefully, and the box moved slightly backwards and forwards, in order that the article is lit to its best advantage. Remember that any cutting or engraved decoration has to be recorded with as much contrast as possible, and even a very small movement or change of angle can make a material alteration in the appearance of the final print.

The determination of the exposure is the next matter to be decided. If a straight reading is taken from the camera position, the mass of dense blackness around the item will cause the camera or other meter to be misled, and lead to the photograph being very much over-exposed. Here, a professional photographer would use a 'grey card' held in the plane of the item being recorded, and use the exposure reading off that in making the exposure. If the photographer has such a card, then he will of course use it, but those less well equipped could with almost equal accuracy take a similar exposure reading from the inside surface of a standard brown manila envelope, or fall back on the original method used in these circumstances, and take the requisite reading from two hands held in front of the object. It is as well to remember that no matter how modern or sophisticated the camera being used, it will not accurately determine exposure under these circumstances without some assistance from its user! It may indeed be as well to 'bracket' the final exposure; this means to expose a sequence of shots, giving initially the determined exposure, then secondly one with one stop more, then one with one stop less exposure than the initial exposure. Some modern and sophisticated cameras have a bracketing sequence mode built into their automated systems, and if available, this can also be used.

Many people have experienced difficulty in photographing pieces of coloured glass, especially of the ruby or blue (Bristol) types. However, these can successful be photographed by using a reversal of the method outlined above. A white background should be used, with the item of coloured glass standing some ten to fifteen inches (250 to 375mm) in front of the rear of the background used. A large overhead light, or one smaller one at each side, should be arranged to shine in such a way as to illuminate strongly the background rather than the object itself. The reflected light from the background travelling through the glass to the camera will be sufficient to reveal both the shape and the colour of the object. As one might expect, however, if

OPPOSITE PAGE: Fig. 10A (TOP) A cut-glass ewer photographed in available light at set station.
Fig. 10B (BOTTOM) The same ewer photographed using a black painted carton as a shadow-box.

left to its own measuring system, the camera will underexpose the film as it will be unduly influenced by the brightness of the background surrounding the object being recorded, rather than correctly estimating the light that has travelled through the glassware. In this case, a correct exposure will be assured by again bracketing the exposure, and this time the second exposure should be made by opening the lens by one stop, and a further stop for the third. If the photographer (or an automatic camera) has already selected a fairly large aperture, the second exposure can be made by doubling the time the shutter is open, and the third exposure by quadrupling the shutter time; an automatic camera should either be used in an auto-bracketing mode if available, or a manual exposure mode be selected, and the necessary adjustments be made to suit.

The essential points therefore in photographing glassware are:

❑ Preferably use a shadow box, or black painted carton, as described.
❑ The light used should be from one side at an oblique angle, and *not* frontal.
❑ Care needs to be taken in making small adjustments in angle and position of item to achieve the maximum contrast as seen through the camera viewfinder.
❑ Correct exposure should be calculated by using a grey card or alternative.
❑ Exposures should ideally be bracketed.

■ Stained glass windows

Throughout this guide so far the approved film recommended is a medium speed colour negative type (for prints), but there is no doubt that many recorders prefer using a positive type film (for slides) when photographing stained glass windows. However, if a complete photographic record of a church's furnishings is being undertaken, with the majority of prints being taken with colour negative film type, then the windows should be similarly recorded. Ideally, the windows can if necessary be photographed both ways, to give prints for the *Church Property Register* record, and slides if there is a strong personal preference for them. Certainly many repairers of stained glass would prefer slides as a reference to the colours of the original glass, and this should be borne in mind when making a choice, if only one set of records is to be made. On the other hand, if the *Register* is being examined for a general reference, then having to use a viewer or projector to see the window detail when all the other records are available in print form is an added inconvenience.

Whatever film type is being used, the method is similar. Deciding when to photograph a window is a matter of waiting for the right weather conditions, for although the camera is of course used to record the inside of the glass from inside the church, the light used for the photograph must come from outside the window in order that it shines through the glass to reveal the colour and the detail. Therefore the light inside the window must be less than the light outside it; while this may seem glaringly obvious, one still finds photographers using a camera-mounted flash unit when photographing a stained glass window. Of course, there must be no artificial light source illuminating the glass from the inside. Also, avoid an unclouded sun shining directly on to the window, for this will lead to great exposure difficulties as one part of the window can be very much brighter than another. Ideally, choose a 'bright cloudy day', that description found on film wrappers as an exposure guide for almost as long as there has been film. In other words, a day when broken clouds cover the sun itself for most of the time, but not a day when thick unbroken cloud makes one wonder whether to wear a raincoat!

Windows will be the largest items that are generally individually recorded photographically in a church, and although an overall photograph should be taken of the entire window, this will not show the detail on each panel sufficiently well to use the photograph on its own. Other photographs showing individual characteristics will need to be taken; it is essential that sufficient notes are taken at the time to enable

OPPOSITE PAGE: FIG.11A (TOP) Stained-glass window photographed with a standard 50mm lens, with the camera set up too close to the actual window, resulting in obvious distortion.
FIG.11B (BOTTOM) Use of a longer focus lens well away from the window results in little distortion.

each detail photograph to be identified correctly as coming from a particular window. When taking the overall photograph, do not be tempted to use a wide-angle lens, for this will undoubtedly cause the window's image to be quite distorted, especially if the camera was in any way tilted in order, for example, to include the topmost part of the window in the shot. It is far better to use a standard or longer focus lens, with the camera set up on its tripod, some distance from the window being photographed.

The tripod used should be as high as possible, consistent with its stabilty; the use of a cable release or similar is essential, especially if a longer focus lens is used. The exposure used is also not as straightforward as one might think, for a camera's built-in automatic exposure meter will be easily fooled into making an incorrect exposure. If the camera has a spot-metering facility, this should be used, and an average calculated after taking several readings of the dark and the lighter areas. As a general guide, give a somewhat shorter exposure than indicated if the window appears dark, and a longer exposure if the window appears to be bright. Experience here is really necessary, but if in doubt, bracket the exposures as explained earlier. It is as well to remember that transparency films have much less latitude than negative types, and require a much more accurate exposure than print film.

One way of lighting and photographing stained-glass windows that was popular some years ago, and one used with success by the author, is to set up the camera and focus as normal inside the church late in an evening, or at night, and then select a medium aperture and open the shutter as for a time exposure. Then, leaving the camera, go outside the church and fire off a number of open flashes from a powerful flash-gun at a distance from the window being photographed. Alternatively, 'paint' the outside of the window with light from a portable floodlight – this method is used by television companies for such programmes as 'Songs of Praise'. It is suggested that should the photographer attempt to use this method, some experiments or practice be made before finalising the procedure.

To sum up then, the main points to be borne in mind when recording stained glass windows are:

❑ On no account use any form of artificial lighting inside the window.

❑ Choose a cloudy but bright day for the photographs.

❑ If possible use a long-focus lens, and set the camera up some distance away.

❑ Calculate the exposure with care, and if in doubt, bracket it to give several shots.

❑ Record the detail in several exposures after the entire window has been taken.

■ Paintings

Paintings do not appear in great numbers in churches, but many places of worship have one or two, and very often, paintings of hitherto unknown value are discovered in them. It is therefore essential that all items are photographed, even if at the time they are thought to be worthless or of little religious value. The vast majority of these paintings are oils, and may or may not be glazed. Whether they are or not, do not attempt to photograph them using any form or flash lighting; even a varnished but unglazed painting will act as an excellent reflector! There is no doubt that the best method of photographing any painting is to use good natural lighting outdoors on a cloudy but bright day; this will ensure a good overall exposure and an accurate rendition of the actual colours present in the painting. But it is appreciated that many paintings found in churches are too large or too high or too firmly attached to the fabric to be moved easily.

When photographing a painting in situ, it is vital that the camera is supported on its tripod at a height equal to the centre of the picture; if this is not possible, then use a longer focus lens, and set up the camera some distance away from the painting in order to minimize any possible distortions to its shape due to tilting the camera. As mentioned in the section on windows, it is also a mistake to use a wide-angle lens close to a painting in order to simplify the composition in the camera viewfinder. Once the painting is in focus, calculate the exposure settings, using if necessary a fairly wide aperture as the depth of focus needed will be slight. Again, if in doubt, make several bracketed exposures to ensure getting one shot correctly exposed. If the painting is in a very dark position, try lighting it softly using a small portable and fairly low-powered lamp angled upwards some distance in front of the painting, so that no direct light may cause unwanted reflections. It will only require a very little extra light to make an appreciable difference to the apparent brightness of the subject to the camera lens.

Should the painting be glazed, it may be found that try as the photographer might, it is impossible to avoid unwanted and obvious reflections appearing even in the camera viewfinder. If visible here, they will be very much more noticeable in the final print! It will be found that the only practical way to remove these reflections prior to the exposure being made is by use of a double polarizing filter mounted on to the camera lens after the shot has been composed, and the lens focused. This filter has two glass discs, one fixed and mounted nearest to the camera, and a second that is capable of being rotated, on the outside of the mount. In use, the photographer looks through the camera viewfinder, and carefully rotates the outside disc of the filter. It will be seen that the reflections are altered according to the position of the rotating filter, and the position that removes most of the visible reflections should be chosen. This filter has a number of drawbacks: first, it is expensive to purchase, especially in the larger sizes. Second, its use will considerably lengthen the exposure shutter time necessary, as it does cut down the light passing through it considerably; this effect differs according to the position of the rotating element in front of the fixed element. The camera's built-in through the lens meter will of course compensate for this light loss. As an aside, this type of filter does have another very beneficial use, in that it is the only way to improve the sky contrast on a colour film, by darkening the blue part of the sky, without affecting in any way the apparent colours of other parts of a landscape. If the photographer engages in this type of work, the cost of the filter will be offset by its more frequent use. When selecting a polarising filter, do not be tempted to purchase a cheaper type called a 'linear' polariser, as this will not enable unwanted reflections to be controlled.

If possible, the rear of any painting recorded should also be closely examined, and any labels, writing or numbers that appear on the frame, stretcher, or canvas or panel, should be photographed in close-up. Many such numbers can be recognised by an expert as being placed there by one of a number of auction houses, museums or cataloguers in the past and can be of the utmost assistance in enabling such an expert to determine a painting's origin and value. A golden rule to be remembered by all recording photographers is 'If in doubt – don't leave it out'. The cost of an additional exposure and print is only a few pence, but its inclusion can often save many pounds later.

It will be seen therefore, that the points to be remembered are:

❏ Try and get the painting to appear as truly 'square' as possible, by using a longer lens.
❏ Either angle the painting slightly to remove reflections, or use a polarising filter.
❏ Do not use a flash unit; if needed, use a small lamp angled upwards from the front, and some distance away from the painting.
❏ Record all details on the rear of the painting or frame.

■ Textiles

Church textiles such as tapestries, carpets, vestments, altar cloths, hangings, kneelers, banners and flags are all worthy subjects for the recording camera, but they are all too often overlooked. Because of the general non-reflectance of textile materials, it is one of the few subjects which can confidently be photographed with the aid of a flash unit. The whole of an object should be recorded, even if it is quite large. Carpets for example can be spread out on the floor under an organ loft or other elevated position if possible, and photographed from above so that the entire carpet area is recorded and the carpet itself is thus photographed with as little distortion as possible. Very large altar carpets of course cannot be dealt with in this way, and can be photographed where they lie, but some detail shots will be needed to show the patterning and texture of the carpet.

Vestments and altar cloths can also be photographed, again, if possible, to show their entirety; damaged and repaired areas should be separately recorded in a close-up photograph. Many textile objects in churches are too fragile to be disturbed unduly – one is used to seeing banners and flags hanging as memorials or as armorials, and these especially can be damaged if moved after years of exposure to light and dust. They will have to be photographed in their permanent positions, and the photographer should consider using a long focus lens and setting up his camera at some distance from the item in order to lessen the distorted perspective that may result if an attempt is made too near to it. The flash unit being used may not have sufficient power or covering width to cope with this increased distance, and recourse will have to be made either to using an extended time exposure, or using a floodlight or portable video light referred to earlier.

Do not fall into the temptation of taking short cuts when recording such items as altar cloths and other larger items. Some years ago a very early and highly valuable table carpet used on an altar in a remote rural church was reported as stolen. The church authorities concerned had not photographed the item individually, but had relied on an overall shot of the altar decorated for an Easter celebration as being sufficient. It was only after over twenty hours of work by an extremely competent photographer that a print of sufficient quality was obtained to give the investigating police a picture of some of the patterning and detail of the item in order for publicity to be obtained. The item was eventually recovered directly as a result of the small detail photograph being shown on a national television programme. It is very doubtful if today any police force would have either the finance or expertise available to enable it to spend so much time in obtaining a photograph to use in an investigation – a photograph that in any event should have formed part of the inventory of the church concerned! It cannot be emphasised too strongly that all the furnishings found in a church should be individually photographed; if in doubt, don't leave it out.

A short list of the main points to be remembered are:

❑ Flash units of sufficient power can safely be used.
❑ Try and record items without distortion to perspective by not tilting camera.
❑ Record in close-up all areas of damage or repair.
❑ Do not omit any item, no matter how apparently insignificant or unimportant, and do not be tempted into believing that the item might be included in a shot of another nearby object.
❑ While the reference number may not be included on the item when it is photographed, have sufficient written notes for later identification to be certain.

■ Carvings

As all types of carvings have become popular as house furnishings as well as being items of an antique interest, so their theft from churches has increased. Both stone and wood carvings should be photographically recorded, even when they are considered as part of the church fabric and structure; relief stone panels mounted on a church wall, memorials, and carved decorative finials on a rood screen, and on pews, have all been recorded as being stolen in recent years. While flash photography can often be used, great care should be exercised if the item concerned has any form of polished or painted finish, as with these a greater or lesser amount of flash flare or reflection will occur. A bounced flash technique will often simplify exposure lighting, if the photographer has both the equipment and the experience to enable this to be undertaken. Alternatively, a clip-on diffuser can often be obtained for individual flash units, and these can also assist the photographer in obtaining a glare-free result.

However, some relief carved panels, and incised decorations and inscriptions on panels may appear as flat and undetailed impressions if plain flash lighting is used. Better results will be achieved if some form of bulb lighting is used in a deep metal shade held at one side of the panel, so as to throw into sharp contrast the carving or inscription. Many very shallow inscriptions can be lit easily to give very impressive results, if the shade is held at one side of the panel and one edge raised a small amount, so that the light spills at a shallow and acute angle across the area being recorded. In many cases the edge of the shade may need to be raised by as little as five to ten millimetres, in order for the panel to spring into view in a manner that is often more legible than it is normally seen.

Carvings, especially free-standing figures, also benefit, photographically speaking, by being recorded with the light stronger from one side than the other, so as to accentuate the modelling detail of the piece. Only a very subtle difference in intensity from one side to the other may be found necessary; it may help to know that the human eye can easily differentiate about two thousand shades of a colour, but at best a colour film can only record eighty or so. So whilst a figure may be seen by the eye as being gently modelled in whatever light is falling on it, some alteration may be needed to enable the film to record the modelling. With plain stone and marble carvings this is especially difficult. It is all too easy to find on the final print that what the photographer originally thought was a very beautiful face on a carved figure has been reproduced as a featureless white blob.

While not 'carvings' as such, decorated organ pipes of both wood and metal have been stolen for use as decorative items, so again, photographs of these may not only assist in their recovery, but can also help in the production of replacements if this should unfortunately be required.

❏ Flash may be used, but bounced or angled flash may give better results.

❏ Carved relief or incised items should be lit from an angle.

❏ Shallow incised or engraved details are best lit from a very shallow angle, by a bulb in a deep shaded holder.

■ Furniture

Furniture is perhaps one of the easier types of church furnishing to record photographically, but there are a few special points to be borne in mind. The use of a background cloth suitably suspended behind a piece of furniture will isolate it from what may well be an otherwise confusing background, and also help to give a more 'professional' finish to the appearance of the final prints. The cloth background need not be an elaborate item in itself – one recorder uses two clothes props with a bean stick supported horizontally between them to hold the cloth, giving the finished prints all the appearance of carefully posed studio shots! Make sure, however, that the cloth used is carefully selected; a plain and pastel coloured one is preferable to a coarsely woven and patterned one. The difference that can be achieved in the appearance of a photograph of an item of furniture taken in situ, with a little extra care, can be seen in Fig. 12.

OPPOSITE PAGE: FIG. 12A (TOP) Chair photographed *in situ*, with confusing background.
FIG. 12B (BOTTOM) Photographed against a cloth held on a slide screen behind item.

While most examples photographed can be safely lit using a flash unit, beware if a good polished surface is present, as it is all too easy to get a burnt-out area on the item's surface caused by reflectance of the flash source. As previously mentioned, this can be negated if a bounced flash technique or a diffused flash is used. However, if the photographer is not so equipped, or does not have the necessary experience, it may be advisable to avoid the use of flash, and either use a floodlight or video lamp reflected off a wall or ceiling, or fall back on the safest method, available light. As a further consideration, it is quite possible to light large items (or areas) by 'painting' them with light from a portable source. The lamp should be moved back and forth, up and down, so as to cover the area required without any missed areas, overlapping the edges of the beam with each movement. In this way, the item can be evenly lit, and because the light falls upon it from a number of different angles, only very soft shadows, if any, will be produced. In the past, even light from hand torches has been used in this manner, and a whole interior illuminated by the light from a paraffin fuelled pressure lamp. It may be as well though, to practise these techniques before relying on one or two attempts when actually on a recording assignment.

Again, when photographing an item of furniture, record in close-up areas of damage, and restored and repaired areas. Additionally, there are often areas of interest inside, behind, or beneath the piece being photographed – it is often the attention to these areas that can prove of so much value for reference purposes in the longer term.

While the recording of furniture is one of the easier subjects, there are still some essential points to remember:
- ❑ While flash can be used, a softened or diffused flash is often better.
- ❑ Isolate items from their surroundings with a suitably supported plain cloth.
- ❑ Record in detail areas of damage, repair or restoration.

■ General hints

Although it was originally stated in this guide that the ideal recording method is to have a central station to which items can be brought to be photographed, there are many places where to do so may not be practicable; or many items may be too heavy or considered too valuable. In these situations the camera has to be taken to the subject, and it is under these circumstances that the advantages of having the camera mounted on a good, firm tripod are most apparent. As a general rule, the camera should be placed in front of the item, with the lens on a central line with the front of the item in such a way that ideally there is no need for the camera to be tilted up or down, or angled, while the composition and focusing are completed. The now common practice of only owning a zoom lens with a camera may enable some flexibility to be accepted in the camera positioning while still enabling the composition to fill the available negative area. However, their use is at the expense of a lower light transmission, and some apparent distortion, when compared with even an inexpensive fixed focal length lens. The photographer must balance the flexibility of a zoom lens with the very superior light transmission and definition under exacting conditions that can be achieved by a standard prime lens. Currently, the price of a good medium range zoom lens having an effective maximum aperture of f3.5 to 5.6 (according to the position in the zooming range chosen) costs about the same as a high quality 50mm f1.4 lens of the same make. The performance of the 50mm lens at its maximum aperture will be superior to that of the zoom lens set to the same focal length and used at its maximum aperture; the former may well be transmitting eight times as much light as the zoom lens, which not only simplifies focusing in poor lighting, but also materially helps to make life easier when it comes to making the actual exposure. In this, as in most things, one pays one's money and takes one's choice. Before leaving this topic, it will be seen that even when the camera is moved around from subject to subject, there will be a definite improvement both to the artistic composition and in obtaining a standard exposure

setting, if the same background material is used behind each item. Achieving a balanced and standard procedure will not only enable a large number of items to be recorded at one session, but will also help to produce a standard style to the group of finished prints, and an overall impression of real professionalism.

Of course, each item being photographed, either in situ or at a set station, should as far as possible fill the frame in the camera viewfinder. It is of little use making an artistic composition and correctly focusing and exposing the camera, if the item in the finished print appears as a minute image amid a large area of bland stonework, or background cloth! So often one finds that detail in such photographs can only be seen with the aid of a magnifying glass.

When photographing large, free-standing, polished items such as brass eagle lecterns, floor-standing candlesticks, and even well polished wooden items, the techniques for dealing with unwanted reflections and highlights, as detailed in the section dealing with photographing silverware, are equally valid. A few dabs with a ball of softened 'Plasticine' can make all the difference between an adequate photograph and a superb one.

Do not be afraid of making time exposures, as the technique can considerably extend the usefulness of your camera. Many modern electronically controlled cameras are even equipped to enable this to be done automatically, with shutters programmed to extend the exposure time up to around thirty seconds if needed. The older type of camera has a shutter fitted with a 'T' setting, the letter standing for 'Time'; to use this facility, a good smooth cable release is required. A difference in an exposure due to a miscalculation of say, 1/250th second instead of one of 1/125th is equivalent to an error of one stop, or 100 per cent; a difference in exposure between one of eight seconds and one of sixteen seconds is about a third of a stop, or 33 per cent. This 'error' is within the exposure latitude of a modern colour negative film, although of course we should always aim at obtaining a truly correct exposure. The smaller difference than expected is because of the way that a long exposure in a dim light affects a film emulsion, which is quite different from the way it is affected by a shorter exposure in a brighter light. Without delving too far into the mathematics and theory of this, it does mean that for practical purposes it is difficult to overexpose a film during a time exposure. To photograph the whole of the interior of a particular church may require an exposure of 1/60th second with the help of a dozen or so flash-guns, and fifteen seconds when photographed with no additional lighting. There will not be an unusable result if the exposure was inadvertently extended to, say, 25 seconds! A longer exposure of a church's interior may indeed produce a more attractive result than a shorter artificially lit one, for there would be no hard shadows, an evenness of lighting, and perhaps, with luck, a few convenient and artistic sunbeams shining down into the nave. Similarly, a photograph of a large piece of furniture taken with a short exposure using a flash or floodlamp may well give hard shadows and undue reflections, while a naturally lit exposure of a few seconds' duration produces an attractive picture without any difficulty. Do not disregard the assistance to an exposure that even a plain white card reflector can give, for its use can often more than halve an exposure time; the use of a mirror surface on a smaller item can reduce an exposure dramatically.

4

Storage of prints and negatives

This part of the guide deals with points most often overlooked - the correct and safe storage of your prints and negatives. It is of no use taking a lot of trouble and expending sums of money in producing a complete photographic record of the furnishings of a church, if the prints and negatives are to be placed en masse in the drawer of a convenient sideboard or desk. Nothing will cause greater damage to your work than the effect of dampness, however slight, on the negatives; this form of storage will quickly produce growths of a fungus on the emulsion surface, and the damage is permanent and irreparable. Also, negatives kept together in the wallet in which they were returned from the processors can produce damage caused by scratching, and again, the damage is permanent, and can make reprinting both difficult and useless.

Negatives should be correctly stored in an album sold for that purpose at reasonable cost; at the time of writing (1996) a negative album with sufficient storage capacity for sixty films retails at less than £10, an inconsiderable sum to pay for the safe and permanent storage of around fourteen hundred individual negatives. Negatives should not be cut into individual parts, but should be stored in the short strips returned from processing; the storage album has pages consisting of sleeves to facilitate this. Do not handle negative surfaces with bare fingers; hold the strips by the edges only. Even an apparently dry finger will leave sufficient moisture on even a fleeting touch to make an almost indelible, and fungoid producing, fingerprint. The negative strips can be indexed for rapid access, using index pages supplied with the majority of these special albums.

Lastly, do not attempt to save money by storing negatives in common envelopes, as the paper from which they are manufactured has an acidic content; this can attack the chemical composition of the film emulsion quite quickly, leading to puzzling changes in colour balance in prints produced later.

Prints should be mounted in albums sold for the purpose, although the 'self-adhesive' types are better avoided. Although convenient, the transparent overlay can cause problems later when an individual print may be required for reproduction or serious study. It is often found that even after only a year or so, it may be impossible to remove a print without tearing it, or creasing or scratching its surface. Any such damage renders the print useless for either type of use, and will cause a delay while a replacement print is produced from the negative. Also, the transparent overlay can cause air bubbles to form over the print surface, and also can lead to fungus growth, and discoloration. An older type of album requiring gummed mounting corners is a better storage system, if somewhat time-consuming to use. If the expense can be met, there are a number of display albums available with pages made of thin transparent slip-in sleeves of various sizes, both to hold and display prints of various standard sizes; these are both convenient and safe for the long-term storage of valuable prints.

OPPOSITE PAGE: FIG. 14 A print made from a carelessly and incorrectly stored negative, showing scratches and scuff marks. The fingerprint cannot be removed from the negative surface, being etched into the emulsion. This print is useless for any serious purpose.

Appendix 1

This is a list of examples of the main manufacturers' manual focusing cameras available on the second-hand market; the prices quoted are for good, clean examples seen in provincial dealers in January 1996. All the samples listed were offered with a guarantee of between three and twelve months, and are of types that were being manufactured in December 1985, and are thus all ten-plus years old.

Make & model	Type details	Price
Zenith EM	Manual exposure 35mm SLR of Russian manufacture	£34
Pentax MG	Automatic aperture priority exposure, with Pentax 50mm f2 lens	£75
Ricoh XR7	Manual and automatic aperture priority exposure, with 50mm f2 lens	£90
Pentax ME Super	Manual and aperture priority automatic exposure, with 50mm f1.7 lens	£110
Pentax K1000	Manual exposure, with 50mm f2 lens. Solidly built and popular model	£120
Olympus OM1n	Manual exposure, with 50mm f1.8 lens	£125
Canon AE1	With programmed, aperture priority, and manual exposure modes. With 50mm f1.8 lens	£135

Olympus OM2	Automatic aperture priority exposure with reading off film plane. With 50mm f1.8 lens	£145
Canon A1	With programmed, aperture, and shutter priority exposure modes, and manual. With 50mm f1.8 lens	£180
Nikon FM2	Manual exposure system, with f1.4 lens	£380
Canon F1n	Versatile pro-type camera, with manual exposure mode, and fitted with f1.8 lens	£485

Appendix 2

This is a list of new manual focusing 35mm SLR cameras available in January 1996. The prices quoted are the average retail prices from provincial dealers.

Make & model	Type details	Price
Zenith 122K	Russian-made camera with f2 lens, and standard Pentax K mount	£90
Vivitar V3000	Manual exposure, with 50mm f1.7 lens	£100
Yashica FX-3 Super	Manual exposure, with 50mm f2 lens	£150
Centon DF300	Aperture priority automatic and manual exposure. With 50mm f2 lens	£155
Praktica BX20S	Automatic and manual exposure, with 50mm f1.8 lens. Made in former East German factory, recently re-opened	£185
Ricoh KR10m	Aperture priority and manual exposure modes. With 28 – 70mm zoom lens	£225
Pentax P30T	Automatic programmed exposure and manual, with 35 – 80mm zoom lens	£240
Pentax K1000	Long-lived popular manual camera, with 50mm f2 lens	£250

Minolta X700	Well-made aperture priority and manual exposure model. With 50mm f1.7 lens	£380
Ricoh XRX-3PF	Multi-exposure modes, with 28 – 80mm zoom lens	£400
Nikon FM2n	Pro-type manual exposure camera, with 50mm f2 lens	£630
Contax 167 MT	Quality camera with automatic/manual exposure modes. Fitted with German-made 50mm f1.7 lens of highest quality	£778

Note: Should an automatically focusing camera be required, readers are advised to visit any dealership, and inspect personally. There are a great many models and types available, ranging in price from £250 to £1500. Prime 50mm lenses are usually an extra.